MIDDLETOWN

STEPHANIE ROGERS

Distributed by Independent Publishers Group

©2025 Stephanie Rogers

No part of this book may be used or reproduced in any manner without written permission except in the case of brief quotations embodied in critical articles and reviews. Please direct inquiries to:

Saturnalia Books
2816 North Kent Rd.
Broomall, PA 19008
info@saturnaliabooks.com

ISBN: 978-1-947817-86-9 (print), 978-1-947817-87-6 (ebook)
Library of Congress Control Number: 2025930813

Cover art and book design by Robin Vuchnich

Distributed by:
Independent Publishing Group
814 N. Franklin St.
Chicago, IL 60610
800-888-4741

Contents

In Middletown, the Summers Wept	3
A Minor Key	4
After Wine, I Think of My Father	5
Baptism	6
Stephanie, Heather, and Ian: Ohio, 1986	7
Smallest House on the Street	9
That Moon Again	10
What a Kid	12
The Moon Never Did Me Any Favors	13
Learning to Play the Oboe	14
Clover	16
Dear Sister of My Childhood	17
On the One-Year Anniversary of My Father's Death	19
Tornado: A Warning	20
Chip's Laundromat	22
The Bee Sting	23
I Should've Loved My Parents But They Scared Me	25
Warning to My Parents Thirty Years Too Late	26
The Storm	28

Self Portrait Through My Brother's Eyes	32
Ian Vignettes	33
Bullet	37
Apology to My Parents Thirty Years Too Late	38
Self Portrait Through My Sister's Eyes	39
I Once Asked My Father Where I Should Bury Him	41
After My Father's Service	42
Leaving Cincinnati	43
I Dream My Father Back	47
The Good Daughter	49
Ode to Insomnia	51
White Trash Eulogy	52
One Last Poem for My Mother	53
A Bird That Flies Over the Dead	54
Suppose You Happened	55
Acknowledgments	59
Author Bio	61

For Heather and Ian

In Middletown, the Summers Wept

their misty nights over every crevice. I was seven years old, dancing in the yard,
> grass blades moving in the breeze

along with me. It was time for dinner, McDonald's
> and I thought I heard

my mother calling. But she never called. A fire
> ant crawled inside

my pant leg and I screamed, imagining all the places
> it could linger. I stomped

my foot, watched the ant's body wriggle down, then pressed it between
> my fingers until a star flattened against me. It reminded me of how

I thought I heard God once. When I told
> my parents God had whispered

into my ear a hymn
> I didn't know the name of, my father laughed, clipped

chuckles with his head thrown back. My mother never knew what to make
> of me. I thought she hated me

for dumping the liquor down the sink, flushing
> the weed. But it wasn't the night yet.

It wasn't. It wasn't
> the night she threw the Tylenol against my bedroom wall. It wasn't

the night she yelled, *I hope you take a bottle of pills and die.*
> No. That night came later.

A Minor Key

I don't know why I gave my father a pass
for all his fuckups, my mother an eyeroll, the blame.

Maybe I expected her to protect us
like a mother, protect us with her body, a gun

going off, knife blades in the kitchen
ready for a struggle. I didn't know

then that she was human, that she loved me
more than her own mother, her own

father, my father and the never housebroken
pissing dog. I was busy under a blanket

reading *The Amityville Horror* and questioning
how a family lets their demons lurk

in every conversation. Sure, I wanted to get out,
banged my fists against

my bedroom walls and bled. But I stayed. Because
I saw her once after my orchestra concert

standing in the lobby in her floral dress
with sun-rimmed eyes I could tell had been crying.

After Wine, I Think of My Father

    I taste the lip of the glass. The wine goes down like the night I lost
my shoe by throwing it out a car window. Alone, the moon grows old
       up there. People lose things by tossing them out a car window
or cutting open their wrist, so eager to watch the thick Cabernet
       of their insides swirl, reminding them *I'm here*. Last week, I caught
my mother blowing her boyfriend on the living room couch
       and I wondered aloud, *Aren't there better places to open one's mouth
in the dark?* I want to spell out my father's name the way a gravestone
       sheds its chalk when the wind makes a fuss. Steve, who didn't die
from what coursed through the needle. Steve, who barely caught
       the baseball I threw right into the crook of his glove. I want
to remember him the way a bedroom owns a lover, the way a hand
       covers a mouth, muffling the cry. I don't remember why I dropped
my shoe out the car window, except I believed for one night I could fly
       along with it. Steve, who placed his arm so softly around my shoulder,
who smacked his belt against my thigh, sparking the red inside me.

Baptism

        Heather, Ian, and I spent our summers
in a trash can. Dad filled it with water
        from the backyard hose
because the local swimming pool
        cost money and no one had money
        in our part of Middletown. Fired
from sweeping up
        the movie theater, Dad disappeared
into his latest job
        at the video arcade and sometimes
        he brought us those giant sunglasses
that overtook our faces.
        Mom helped fit people for frames
at the optometrist's office
        and every Christmas she read to us,
        everyone surrounding
the tree, the passage from the Bible
        about the resurrection of Jesus.
She always cried. Every summer
        we'd take our naked
        Barbies to the makeshift backyard
water park and hold them
        under the murky black until the almost
drowning, laughing at their soaked hair,
        the dripping from their plastic eyes.

Stephanie, Heather, and Ian: Ohio, 1986

    Ian doesn't look into the camera
but he smiles, hands folded
        in his lap, blond hair browning
at the crown. His blue eyes, pale
        as seawater, seem to breathe.
Almost translucent, they stare,
        two hands skimming a wave, skin
close enough to kiss. I want
        to touch his baby teeth. I should
try to tell him something
        but I haven't yet learned to put words
to violence. Heather sits in front
        of the tin trashcan, sunburnt hair
stringing past her shoulders, yellow
        shirt loose against her neckline.
Arms crossed, knees locked
        together, she gazes dark-eyed into
the lens, sky-kissed shorts cinched
        up her thighs, a ruffled bed sheet.
If I could reach through to touch her
        I'd pretend she were the blooming
petals of a tulip, bring the silk
        to my lips and breathe. How else
to savor a body? I don't recognize
        myself in the pink and blue t-shirt,

cap sleeves, long legs bare
>	like a teenager in a miniskirt, before
I began to pick apart my scars
>	and hide. What is that mid-laugh
mouth, that sure-as-shit kid, exposed
>	tongue taunting the photographer?
Come at us, she seems to say
>	*and see what fucking happens.*

Smallest House on the Street

Our parents either loved or hated us, depending on the year.
      I remember trees
in the yard bending sideways from the earth like arms
stretching out to punch or break
      a heart. Once, my father ripped a wart off
Ian's face. I remember blood down
his chin. I remember leaning against the trees' rough trunks
      to listen to their breathing, the sun beating
across them. I remember grass on a hot day
smelling like rust or lemons. Nights
      when I couldn't sleep, I read about girls
who grew into women and spread apart. I remember cops
showing up on the doorstep after my mother swiped
      a knife at my father, how the wind eased
through the leaves like hair lifted off a woman's long neck.

That Moon Again

I'm stuck inside the airport with a Cabernet and a boyfriend
who won't stop playing Fallout Shelter on his cell phone
and there's that moon again, getting all dirty blonde
behind the clouds, and I can't remember the last time I spoke
to my father before he killed himself
with drugs, we think, though the report
hasn't yet arrived, and I hate my aunt who planned
his memorial service because whoever said I wanted that
song, "Dance with My Father" to play
when honestly I never danced with him in my whole boring life
and I can't get the feeling out
that I did all the wrong things, like maybe
being passed out drunk in a cab when he called me once
and who knows if that talk might've changed things
and I just want it all to stop, so I look at that sky and there I am
again, a child in Dad's wiry arms, my mom
looking on, and isn't she smiling and isn't my anger tamed
finally and isn't the guy who's not yet my boyfriend
somewhere in the universe
not playing Fallout Shelter but waiting for me
to pull my thick bangs back with my glasses and rest
my head on his lap, and when I die will it hurt
the way it hurts to know they found blood on the dishes

in my father's apartment or that he was alone
or that the truth is, the last time I saw him was outside
that McDonald's in Middletown, where he smoked a cigarette
and waved and said, *Hey, Steph,* and my heart sank to look back.

What a Kid

I found out about his death over Facebook Messenger,
some sad-face emoji staring back at me from the screen.
Who does that? I wonder now. No call. No text. Just
an image with a streaming blue tear, something a child
might send. I couldn't believe it. I can't. Who enters
a group chat window, decides to send something a child
might send? Then nothing. Silence. Just my aunt entering
his death into a chat window like something a child
would do, learning her father's gone, not her aunt typing
the news but a child. As his kid, I understand. What a kid:
I loved my father like a child, not an adult absorbing
the news but a child. As his kid, I understand what a kid
would do, learning her father's gone, not her aunt typing
his death into a chat window like something a child
might send. Then nothing. Silence. Just my aunt entering
a group chat window, deciding to send something a child
might send. I couldn't believe it. I can't. Who enters
an image with a streaming blue tear? Something. A child?
Who does that? I wonder now. No call. No text. Just
some sad-face emoji staring back at me from the screen.

The Moon Never Did Me Any Favors

My father took more than his organs
                         with him when he left

and messed up my mind
                         till my own voices sang. Now the sky

darkens the world
                         brunette for a while and I'm unmoved

each minute of it. I try
                         to quiet my grief but it's like a hammer

breaking concrete, my father's body
                         a crushed brick by the dumpster. Now

I'm that fading image
                         in an old Polaroid, a child-creature

reaching for her father's hand, his face
                         diminishing, manholes for eyes.

Learning to Play the Oboe

When I was growing up, the house felt
like a movie projector flashing on
unpainted walls, smoke
from my parents' joint curling
into my lungs, my mother's skillet
bent by a casual toss
to the head of my disobedient
brother, the whack to my sister's back
after our overheard smack talk,
calling our parents
the Drunk-Stoned Wardens of Middletucky
Ohio. Man, the whole lot of us
got depressed, my father ashing his smokes
into the watered-down Crown
Royal glass perched on his knee,
my mother giving up
her twenties for three kids and a secret
coke stash under the bed. And winter
could get nasty
in Ohio, the snow turning dirty as the edges
of a worn Band-Aid. My mom
and I drove the long highway each Saturday
to my Cincinnati oboe lessons
where I spent a season

getting better, accidentally,
than all the high-school oboists a state
could raise. In those days
even if I practiced harder, home
felt like a minor scale I couldn't master.

Clover

Heather, my sister, his youngest girl, his baby—
      the one who always gave in when he needed
money for rent or drugs—left me with her
      three girls outside McDonald's while she drove
Dad for a carton of cigs and a *Playboy*. The girls
      forced me to play freeze tag. I picked
at my fingernails, ripping off a half-moon
      on each hand. The sky sprayed the grass
with sunlight while Sophia and Chloe squashed
      the picnic ants with their tiny fists. I helped
Penny look for clover and when we found
      a four-leafed one, somehow no one cared.
If I could go back, I'd press it into my palm
      and say, *Get ready. Soon they're going to find him*
dead in his apartment across the street. The water
            will be running in the sink.

Dear Sister of My Childhood

Remember Mom and how she sent us away to play near
the highway ditch, us throwing gravel, cracking
a windshield, an accident. The wronged woman dragged us
by the arms, back to Mom, who was talking on the phone

with Dad, their separation not quite official, the whistle
of the kettle in the kitchen. *Listen*, the woman yelled
at Mom who paid attention then. *Your kids banged up
my ride with a rock*, and Mom twisted the phone cord around

her wrist, smiled a *sorry*, sent us to our bedroom where
we blanketed the stuffed animals, planned a fantasy
ship trip and swung them over the green carpet ocean
till a rabbit flew off and drowned, the kittens and bears

unaware of their fallen friend. What the hell? We were fun
kids, placing our heads on Dad's chest, listening for his
heartbeat, our faces like mother birds covering the nest.
We licked our plates clean when told, laughed at the old

dog dragging its ass across the rug, salted up those outdoor
slugs that vanished into mush. Dear sister, visit me now.
New York City stays windy all year, the crowds shouting
their snare-drum quips at one another, the summer sweaty

as beach shells, Dad dead from a rip in the intestine,
Mom's boyfriend gone on the vodka binge and all my life
spent rounding corners like a whirlwind, my smoke
settling now. But here I am, still broke and meddling

in your Nashville life, your three girls sweet as key lime pie
smashed in the face, their tresses long and swaying down
their backs the way honey slips softly from the spoon.
Let's crescendo under the moon together with our banter

misremembering our girlhood just a bit, not flinching
at Dad's belt untwisted from his waist or Mom's glass bowls
thrown and shattered near our faces. Now we're aces, two
women settled and hot as the metal in our teeth drilled out.

On the One-Year Anniversary of My Father's Death

My father watched me bleed once, sliced with a glass shard, foot covered in the warm, the purple. His smile shot through me like a bee, not yet

stinging, waiting. Always wrong, that smile, a Keep Out sign swaying from a child's doorknob. When I looked at him again, my eyes pooling,

the cut not clotting, my fingers sticky with it, my fingers touching my face and staining it, he got down on his knees and grinned. Now his teeth come

back to me like a fading tattoo I can still touch and how, when he finally held me, foot wrapped in his black t-shirt, he said, *One day, you won't even remember*

this happened.

Tornado: A Warning

The storm exhales
inside the clouds. Heather, age 6, runs
down the street, screaming. My mother swipes

Ian off the living room floor, carries him
to the basement. My father jokes
as always because it's funny

to him that Heather, age 6, forgot her Big Wheel
at a friend's house. The storm
eats the face off

a mailbox. Heather runs
down the street, screaming. My mother pushes
Ian's hair off his forehead. I press

my brain against the lone basement window, watch
the storm send the weeds in the yard
flailing. My mother wraps Ian in a blanket

while Heather, age 6, runs
to her friend's house
to retrieve her Big Wheel. My father

licks the inside of a yogurt container
spotless. The storm strips bark from a tree
like some kids peeling the paper off their crayons.

Chip's Laundromat

We walk in on Thanksgiving, trash bags
filled with clothes slung over
our shoulders. Heather insists I break
a twenty at McDonald's. I buy
a dollar cheeseburger, eat it
as the cashier counts out
the nineteen dollars' worth
of quarters. No one else
is there. Neither of us bothers
to separate the whites from colors
or obey the sign that says we shouldn't
sit on top of the washers. So we lie
back, discuss the different shapes
the ceiling stains resemble: butterfly,
atomic bomb explosion, ruffled
curtain, deep red crayon melting down
the wall. We don't want to go home.
Three streets over, our parents wash
the dishes, hit another joint
and pack the leftovers away
while their two daughters hope
the dryers won't really dry the clothes
in fifty minutes. We drag them out.
Heather insists we fold the underwear.

The Bee Sting

I wanted my mother to watch me but Annette, the babysitter, stood
outside instead, squinting into the light around me. I wanted

my father to step out of his car and into the backyard where I twirled
in the new dress Annette had brought, tugging off my corduroy

overalls and lifting my hair off my neck. When it happened at first
I didn't feel it, didn't let it throw me off or change anything at all.

The sky shone down all through it and when I shrieked, Annette
lifted me sobbing off the green and placed me in the gravel driveway.

I whimpered holding a foot bigger to me than the earth crashing into
the sun, couldn't breathe as I watched her move, her quick hands cold

against my skin. She pulled out a pack of Marlboros, the plastic taken
by the wind, and tapped a cigarette on the rocks next to the tube

of Colgate I hadn't seen her grab from the bathroom. She pushed
the paste through and gathered a dime-sized dollop on her pinky finger

careful to twist the cap tight again as if it mattered, my foot buzzing
with what felt like the whole hive in the arch. I didn't understand why

she swept the toothpaste over the sting, tore open her cigarette and let
the tobacco rest on the uneven ground, or why she mixed the brown

stems with the paste, covering the rising wound with a Band-Aid.
I only knew I no longer needed my mother or my father. I needed this

woman who fished for another cigarette, lit it, exhaled and carried me
crying in her arms to the porch swing, whispering *hush*, smelling of ash.

I Should've Loved My Parents But They Scared Me

I swear it wasn't lonely,
        that fear. That they didn't love me. That I could've

walked out the door,
        rain diagonal against me and no one

would've come after me. It was fair
        in a way. Because I should've been better, more

lovable. I should've taken
        my father's hand, bitten down. No.

I was always
        teething. I should've taken

my mother's hand,
        pressed it to my cheek. I'm trying

to say they did what they knew. And what I knew, I took
                          from no one.

Warning to My Parents Thirty Years Too Late

    Silence knows about a father's touch. Silence learns how
to hopscotch the truth
    in childhood. If it weren't for the nighttime I don't know
how I'd know the names for each scar

    climbing my leg like caterpillars clinging to a leaf. No one
knows how to tell a mother
    to dance when she spends
her days trying to wake herself, her mind like so many silk

    headscarves breezing through the wind: how do they sleep
so lonely? I want to jump off
    the circus bus. I want to go back and kiss
my kid-self smack-dab on her blackish coins

    for eyes. No one knows how
to talk about silence, its need to infiltrate
    the body, the body
that wants to dance over death's face and smash

    its eyes like thumbprints inked over lids, an eraser smudge
on paper. In dreams I spin lemons
    from my hands, staining the Bible pages citrus, the pages
clung to by my mother who accidentally raised me

   to believe God doesn't care
how, or if, we figure out our own breathing. Just dance
   I warn her with my black eyes. What does a god want
with children he wouldn't protect

   as children? Sometimes I can hear the answer moving
through my lashes like a baby girl combing
   her doll's thinning hair. Go ahead. Leave me
to my parents. I'll go back there and let my corpse do the talking.

The Storm

I hear music bleeding
from a stranger's

headphones on the train
and I think of that

Pearl Jam song
Joel posted to Facebook

three days before
he killed himself

and I think about
his kids' dog scraping

and chewing her
way under the porch

of their new house,
resting her face near

a puddle, then lapping up
what pink still

bloomed from a sunset.
When my face

reflects back to me
in the train window

along with that
neighborhood coffee

cart tilted up on one
wheel, I hop off

letting the sun break
its neck on the concrete

next to me. I love it
most when the train

beats and drones
against my feet near

the sewers below
and god it's dark

down there like a brain
might feel taking

a boot to the head.
When Heather sent me

a photo of Sophia
who'd written to her

Mommy, *I'm sorry*
Daddy is gone

I refused to cry, listened
instead for six hours

to that one unbroken
light bulb buzzing

above my bathroom
mirror. If only

everything bad
that happened didn't

dredge up all the bad
that came before it.

Some days the thunder
bashes my apartment

window and suddenly
I'm ten years old, hiding

inside the darkest
closet with Heather,

with Ian, convinced
for just one night

we wouldn't die
almost, ever again.

Self Portrait Through My Brother's Eyes

    I sank into the backseat, drew tree trunks
on the fogged window, finger cool on the glass. Mom
      handled the stick-shift. Stephanie flipped off the truckers
when they honked in traffic, each flash of a brake light
        sinking my stomach. Home: three blocks off the Interstate.
Home: the place Dad ran his secret bookie phone line.
      Stephanie leaned the passenger seat back
against my knees, her shoes scuffing the dash. Mom
      backhanded her, red cheek flaming the car's interior afire.
I sketched the trees till they turned to brick,
      the local steel mill surfacing like a flag
surrendered. Mom drove there every day, making
      a home. We hated living there. Dad groped
my girlfriend in the hallway. Mom sucked
      down her mini-thins, mornings spent on the factory line,
her second shift running the register
      at K-Mart. Stephanie stayed in bed those years, her room
in the basement, one window slicing sunlight
      down the wall's chipped paint.

Ian Vignettes

1.

When I think of my father now I'm hidden
under my bed again
with Heather, counting how many times
the belt smacked Ian's thighs: eight, nine.
For coloring rainbows across
his bedroom walls. That's how old he was.

2.

    I often helped my father out of the car
in the parking lot of rehab. Maybe
    that makes someone sick in the head,
doing to a parent what a parent
    should do, but not like when Mom
called the cops on Ian for getting shitfaced
    at sixteen. He spent the night in jail.

3.

We listened at night. Listened to our parents
coughing after each endless drag. Ian tucked
      into his turtle sheets. But sometimes
Dad would laugh when we played
      in the tilted backyard
sprinting toward a tree branch, home plate.
      Home. Where we hid
under beds each time
      the world broke open. Ian. Who laughs
just like him now. Who doesn't
      want to be anything like him, though
he swigs his Bud Light cans,
cigarette dangling just like Dad's, carelessly
      like it could fall at any moment.

4.

Now Ian's a nurse. Fewer panic attacks. Tailgates
at Bengals games. No kids. Divorced twice. Knows how
to make people laugh. Knows how to fuck up
a cigarette. Keeps his gun
holstered on his hip. Plays
a mean video game. Listens but would rather talk. Kills
a six-pack in an hour. Won't drink that fancy shit. Hates
our dead dad. Loves our mom. Pops his pills
                like he learned it from a pro.

Bullet

    I can tell it's coming on because I'm alone again, staring
at the ivory paint peeling from the ceiling like skin
    from a cuticle. When my father died I never spoke
the word *overdose*. But when I found out the real cause,
    accidental, blood washing over his insides, I didn't cry
less hard or feel less like hiding or screaming
    into a t-shirt. Someone tell me why a parent's death
wipes away for a moment all the bad they'd done
    in the world or to children. Like I hated him and now
that he's no longer alive to hate, where does the hate go?
    Maybe it turns into a mouth. It turns into new teeth
fang-like. Or it turns into love, like when he held me
    after I placed my small hand on the not-yet-cooled
stovetop. I remember less my pain than his fear of how
    to take care of his own flesh and blood. Do I miss him?
Not the way I thought I would, with so much chaos
    pooling in my brain, but genuinely and simply, the way
a tear seeps out an eyelid after a long yawn or how
    its shell ticks the ground once a bullet sears the body.

Apology to My Parents Thirty Years Too Late

There was this time in the emergency room
when my mouth swelled up, a handful
of marbles on my tongue. I thought for sure my throat
would clench and the last breath I took
would be next
to my college roommate. I'm afraid
without writing this no one will know
how much your mistakes made me
all weird and capable of shit. Look at me but please
don't give me that look. My moon
in here drips and beams and see, I made her
a character like you and so I lied sometimes about you.
You never showed up
at the emergency room. And still I kept breathing,
the shot the nurse gave me opening me again
like the bloomed flowers I imagined you'd bring me
one day after my oboe recitals. I'm sorry
to tell you I often cried
about things like that, you not
bringing me flowers. But mostly you touched me
with soft hands and so I invented
in this book the moon
for you, a satellite rising and setting every day
on the faces of your children who learned as children
how to breathe without mouths.

Self Portrait Through My Sister's Eyes

Don't joke about that shit. Those are horrible diseases
I say to Stephanie, who always thinks she's dying. I give her a look

like a baseball thrown hard into a glove. *Fuck this*, she says
because she knows I don't believe her, not that I think she's lying

but that I don't believe in dying that much. Like if I pull apart
a four-leafed clover, it's still called clover, you know? I guess

I don't know what that means but if I had to pretend, which I don't
I'd say it means I can't really stand here in this graveyard

filled with so many things that used to be alive and not think about
all the mean still left. I exhale and clench my body and look over

at Stephanie. Stephanie always wants to know shit. She wants
to know why a guy dumped me but doesn't ask, wants to know why

there are so many gravestones with smiley-face shadows. I squat
behind one of those huge statues I guess rich people buy

when their people go missing into the universe, move to keep
the piss from trickling down my thigh and say, *How much do you think*

this thing cost? and what the hell, I hear her fucking whimper.
I'm like the one upset, remember? I keep it to myself. I'm always

talking to myself the way these ghosts around here must talk
to one another when the living stop haunting. She looks back at me

like a little girl might when she gets lost in a department store
then finally finds her mother. I can totally tell how much

she wants to hug me, so I stand up and take it, my arms at my sides
while she squeezes them against me with her entire body.

I Once Asked My Father Where I Should Bury Him

when he died. It was after he was hospitalized,
in recovery, his ileostomy bag still
new and hanging near the bed's metal rail.
The nurses heard me from their spot outside
his room. One rolled her eyes at another.
One's breath caught in her chest.
I had said something wrong. My father
never loved me
the way my mother loved me but he didn't
hesitate to slip me a twenty-dollar bill
or drop me off at the movies
in his Pontiac Fiero. He told me
he wanted a grave
next to his grandmother. Instead I signed
the cremation forms my aunt emailed
four days after he bled to death. I knew
the ashes were meant to keep
the memorial service cheaper
for his father who was rich and never gave
a dime to my dad
but handed me an envelope
at the funeral with a hundred bucks
inside. It was a Christmas present he told me
as I tucked it into the pocket of my sweater.

After My Father's Service

Water splashing up from the sink, curtain in the window
                turning, wind carrying the air into my lungs, throngs

of ants hoarding crumbs near the tub, grout losing
                its luster like a rain gutter, small talk wearing off

in the ether, leather jacket eating my skin, train waking up
                in the nighttime, calendar of owls

roaming the hillside, whisper of a droplet
                on the grass blade, string on the doorknob to knock

the tooth out, deep end of the summer
                house pool, breeze on the highway

cop car sirens, unspooling of the handsewn blanket, split
                skin of the upper lip chapped off, quiet clink

of the scorpion earrings on the dresser, dry cleaner
                who returned my coat, little red heart on the hanger.

Leaving Cincinnati

Cincinnati, I hated you
the way a child
leans into a storm

from a laundromat door,
putting out her tongue
to catch the rain before

her mother yanks her
back to dirty clothes.
You could've

let me be. Instead
you pirouetted on
my forehead. You never

fell. You watched
my father wake up
in a tipped-over recliner,

his nose bloodied
again. You watched me
toss the shirt he wore

the day before across
his face. You dripped
rain like little feet

along the awning.
You watched me answer
the officer: *Sir, this is*

my father, his toes curled
under, his fists
clenched. Was it

a seizure or an orgasm?
It was a holiday
from pulling him out

of the bathwater,
the shoe he used
to smash the nonexistent

spiders floating beside
a pill bottle. Did he take
a couple or a handful?

Cincinnati, I preferred
your nighttime
whispering, not his

near-death nude
hallucinations that
required paperwork:

police, rehab, hospital,
insurance, history
of drug abuse

and mental health.
I wanted all that easy
sucking down of

cappuccinos during
my weekly trips
to buy him groceries,

his case of Bud Light
cans, his Marlboros,
his weed. Everywhere

you breathed
and watched while I
skipped class to break

down in a bathroom stall.
What time was it,
where were my friends,

and who? You were
a two-year tornado
I sleepwalked through,

the boyfriend who says,
She's just a girl I know.
You knew several girls.

I Dream My Father Back

Don't take me down to the dark where the dog perks up at her meat supper.
Watch the blood drip purple off

the incisors, the dream-dog's bird friend
perched above my bed, ceiling red with feather light. I want to

wake up, divide time between the kiss and the *oh*, my heart gone dizzy
as a merry-go-round, brain ground down to mush, my lust

weakening the seams of me. Thanks, new boyfriend, sprinting the hills
to find me ripening beneath

the dream ceiling again. I watch its fire churn like my father's ashes
blazing, the urn loaded up, the boats of my eyes

taking on water. Wake me. The dog
snaps at my toes and who remembers where I stocked my gun? The bird

above me bleats through its beak to quake me with memories
of him: my father running toward me when I clocked

my forehead against a playground pole, the red soup of the cut
dripping, eye socket black, swelling, Dad's palm not sopping up

much. Then the blood got his shirt, dirt
wet with purple humming and the grass sodden with my mess. I miss him

I guess, because dreams plague me every night since he left, my boyfriend
carving my mouth out with his tongue

to help me speak again. Still, the dream-dog raps, the door
to my brain-room cracked and waiting for dark

to prick my heart muscle. Remember? Never not remembering, I dream
I scream down the dark, the dog, the bird's feathers crimson as the snow

that caught the brunt of my head wound,
my father's hands, always his hands, moving over and over to cover the cut.

The Good Daughter

I slap Mom's face. Burned, she dances back stunned
                      into movement as I step over the yawning ocean
we're both about to drown in. I smell the ashes
                      in our latest sky, open my mouth to taste

the gunpowder. I watch Mom's eyes go bloodshot,
                      listen to the air around us exhale a breath
as I clutch my Barbie, rip out her strands of blonde
                      and it sounds like the fistfuls of grass I tore up

once to bury my murdered firefly. Rhonda,
                      my mom, Rhonda sprinting toward me
on the softball diamond when I pitched
                      a no-hitter, Rhonda storming through the halls

of Middletown High School raging
                      at my band teacher, *you better not let these girls
keep bullying my daughter.* We're not really
                      drowning in the ocean. But a hurricane's eye

swells between us. There's a word in Middletown
                      we use when something goes awry—*veace*—bad
thing, ruinous, *I can't believe how veace our parents are,*
                      Heather joked and because we love-hated them

we burrowed into our shame quietly.
        Mom stares into the carpet's green storm
and dips her toe to test my irritation. *Ladybug,*
        Mom called me and I liked the idea of wriggling

on my back, anger-red, spotted black, waiting
        for a stranger to flip me right again. In high school
when I studied Spanish with Mr. Hartmann,
        Mom's same teacher from twenty years before,

she said to me, looking down at my class schedule
        te amo, Ladybug and I, her first daughter, little
insect, favorite oboist out there, smacker of softballs
        over the fence and mothers, yelled back: *fuck you.*

Ode to Insomnia

I hate waking up each night like this, the cockroach crawling through
        the bathroom, my middle-of-the-night magazine-in-hand dance
with it. And worse, last week, hearing that music again
when all else? Silent. Just my boyfriend wheezing in bed next to me,
        his face pillow-smashed, the fan on low but in my ears some song
long enough to warrant the thought, *This is finally it. I've entirely
lost it.* Just last night didn't I stand, the edge of the subway platform
        looming, next train ready to show up, our bodies pumping blood
to our knuckles knowing just one shove would send us all
to the tracks? I don't want to wake up each night to this
        crushed tulip on the nightstand or to wake up thinking about how
my father's ashes will remain in that urn forever
chiseled on front with a basketball hoop. I don't want to die
        like that, no one knowing how to remember me, the whole house
rigged, each room of my life, an empty cord hanging from a phone booth.

White Trash Eulogy

What I understand now
I came away with slowly, my father's sneer
creeping across his face when I showed up
at home with a wide smile and a bouquet
of weeds I'd gathered near
the highway. I was a kid. I wanted to please
him. I didn't know the difference between
the dead and the beautiful or how
it would feel to watch him turn
away, laugh, shut the door, all without
uttering a word. I took the weeds I held
so close to my chest, parked
myself behind the corner
store lot and buried them near a fire
hydrant, their purple petals
crunching and the stems, brittle inside
the earth, cracking underneath the weight
of the dirt. Always now
dead Dad's laughter in my throat
won't quiet, bee's wings motoring away
like a chainsaw. He grew up all cigarette butts
in flowerpots, all Bud Light tallboys
crushed against a forehead. When he visits me
now I tell him *bring me flowers*. I say
next time you take your hands
off my throat, I promise not to scream.

One Last Poem for My Mother

What are you going to do with me this time? And why
        haven't you answered
all my questions? I want to know
        what it feels like to touch you. I want to know
what it looks like
        when you scream. Remember when
I sprayed your white pantsuit with ketchup packets?
        I was a teenager
and didn't know there was anything
        more important than the rose
a boy drew on the back
        of my empty Trapper-Keeper. The thing is
truthfully I love you now and maybe
        always have, so much I want to know
what it felt like
        when you heard that your children's father
bled to death. That it wasn't
        the drugs? That he still
loved you? That the parts of me that are him scare me
        more than the parts of me
                        that are you?

A Bird That Flies Over the Dead

After the rain, a puddle mirrors my distorted
        face. I want to sweep my hand across
the shallow pool, dive through it, my first baptism. God
        help me. I'm still a child eating moonlight.
Like a starving buzzard I devour the carcass.
        Like my mother's hands I reach toward the sky
until nothing comes to save me. Who cares
        what light brings. The wind spins the puddle
into calligraphy. My father collapsed without me,
        without anyone to cradle him. His last breath—
who knows how long it took. I don't know
        what it means to cup a face in my palms,
to say, *I'm nothing without you.* I greet the weeds
        on the side of the highway, all that purple
on brittle sticks. I should eat them, rip up
                the grass beneath me until I reach him.

Suppose You Happened

Suppose nothing woke me and I fell into the green
hole of my body. Suppose you left a note that night.

I never wanted to miss you like I suppose a butterfly
misses her cocoon. If we wanted to dream, suppose

we dreamt together, two drugged-up dancers
snorting snow. Suppose I calmed myself by shaking

tree leaves and no longer wept. How a daughter
hates a father who lives forever screaming. Suppose

no one called about your death. No one called.
No one. Suppose your life meant my red body thought

of nothing like *I want*. Suppose I held you the way
your smoke hovered against the ceiling. Nothing

choked me. I grew into the blue pit of a mouth.
Suppose you lived and the note you never left spits

pieces into the fire. Suppose a tornado meets a stingray
for the first time and sparks. How they remind me

of you, the tracks on your arms an ocean posed
as death. How a father loves a daughter, smooths his

lips against her, wet. Suppose the daughter finds him,
means to kiss him back. What if you saw my face

that night. How I wanted to need you like I suppose
a caterpillar hoards a tulip petal. Suppose we always.

And there were no words from you, just a letting go
of a daughter. Hear me? You let go of a daughter.

Acknowledgments

Many thanks to the editors of the following journals where these poems first appeared, sometimes in different versions:

The Adroit Journal: "I Dream My Father Back"
Another Chicago Magazine: "That Moon Again"
Boulevard: "Bullet"
Exit 7: "The Bee Sting"
Forklift, Ohio: "The Storm"
Hunger Mountain: "Clover"
New Ohio Review: "Chip's Laundromat"; "Dear Sister of My Childhood"
Ninth Letter: "The Moon Never Did Me Any Favors"
The Pinch: "Smallest House on the Street"
The Rupture: "After My Father's Service"; "Tornado: A Warning"
Salamander: "What a Kid"
Third Coast: "Ode to Insomnia"
Tin House: "Learning to Play the Oboe"

This book would not have been possible without the feedback I received in Kathleen Ossip's poetry manuscript workshop at the 92nd Street Y. Thank you to Kathy and my fellow students, particularly Wendy Herbert and Michael Montlack.

Love to Kerri French, who read countless drafts of these poems and who offered support and encouragement as I finished the book and thank you to my poetry mentors who helped with earlier versions: Sandra Beasley, Lynn Melnick, and Maggie Smith.

To Matt Feltman, Kirk Boyle, Chris Culwell, and Joe Gartrell, my deepest gratitude for your friendship in the best and worst times. And endless thanks to Amber Leab, my whole heart.

Thank you to Robin Vuchnich for the incredible cover design, and special thanks to Kathy Fagan, Eugenia Leigh, and Matthew Lippman for their words, kindness, and wisdom.

Endless gratitude to my Saturnalia family, especially Henry Israeli, for believing in this book, for bringing it to life, and for putting it out in the world.

Thank you to my siblings, Heather and Ian, who went through it with me: I wouldn't be here without your unconditional love and laughter.

To my mother: please know that the poems in this book come from a place of love, that I know damn well I wouldn't have become a poet at all without your encouragement and unwavering support of me and my work. Thank you for that. I love you.

To my nieces, Sophia, Chloe, and Penelope: I don't think you'll ever know how much the three of you inspire me. Thank you for slaying.

For Josh, my husband, best friend, favorite person, my soul, I adore you. Your love for this book made me believe in it too, and I'm forever grateful.

Author Bio

Stephanie Rogers is the author of *Middletown* (2025), *Fat Girl Forms* (2021), and *Plucking the Stinger* (2016), all published by Saturnalia Books. She grew up in Middletown, Ohio and was educated at The Ohio State University and the University of Cincinnati. Her work has appeared or is forthcoming in *Georgia Review, Poetry Northwest, Shenandoah, New Ohio Review,* and elsewhere. She lives outside of Nashville in Lebanon, TN.

Also by Stephanie Rogers

Plucking the Stinger

Fat Girl Forms

Middletown was printed in Adobe Caslon Pro

www.saturnaliabooks.org

www.ingramcontent.com/pod-product-compliance
Lightning Source LLC
Chambersburg PA
CBHW060540080526
44586CB00012B/804